"Look deep into nature, and then
you will understand everything better."

Albert Einstein

A shrew eats 80–90% of its body weight in food daily.

Observe
Marvel at every encounter with nature, from the tiny ladybug to the mighty whale, and from the deep sea to the Aurora Borealis.

Inquire
Step into the role of narrator for each visual story, engaging the brain, igniting the imagination, and inspiring further discovery.

Wonder
From an animal that uses a "scarf" to another that uses an "umbrella," nature has an uncanny ability to amaze and astound.

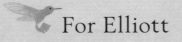

For Elliott

360 DEGREES, an imprint of Tiger Tales
5 River Road, Suite 128, Wilton, CT 06897
Published in the United States 2016
Originally published in Great Britain 2016 by Caterpillar Books
Text by Thomas Hegbrook
Text copyright © 2016 Caterpillar Books
Illustrated by Thomas Hegbrook
Illustrations copyright © 2016 Caterpillar Books
ISBN-13: 978-1-944530-01-3 • ISBN-10: 1-944530-01-0
Printed in China • CPB/1800/0520/0316
All rights reserved • 10 9 8 7 6 5 4 3 2 1

For more insight and activities, visit us at www.tigertalesbooks.com

Every picture tells a story. What do *you* think that story is?

StoryWorlds
NATURE

CREATED BY THOMAS HEGBROOK

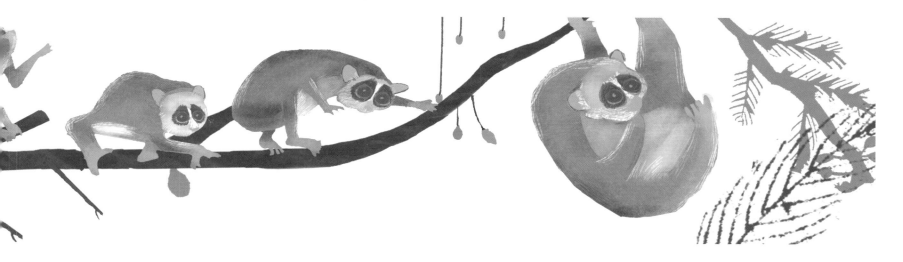

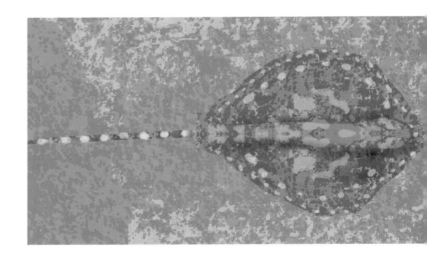

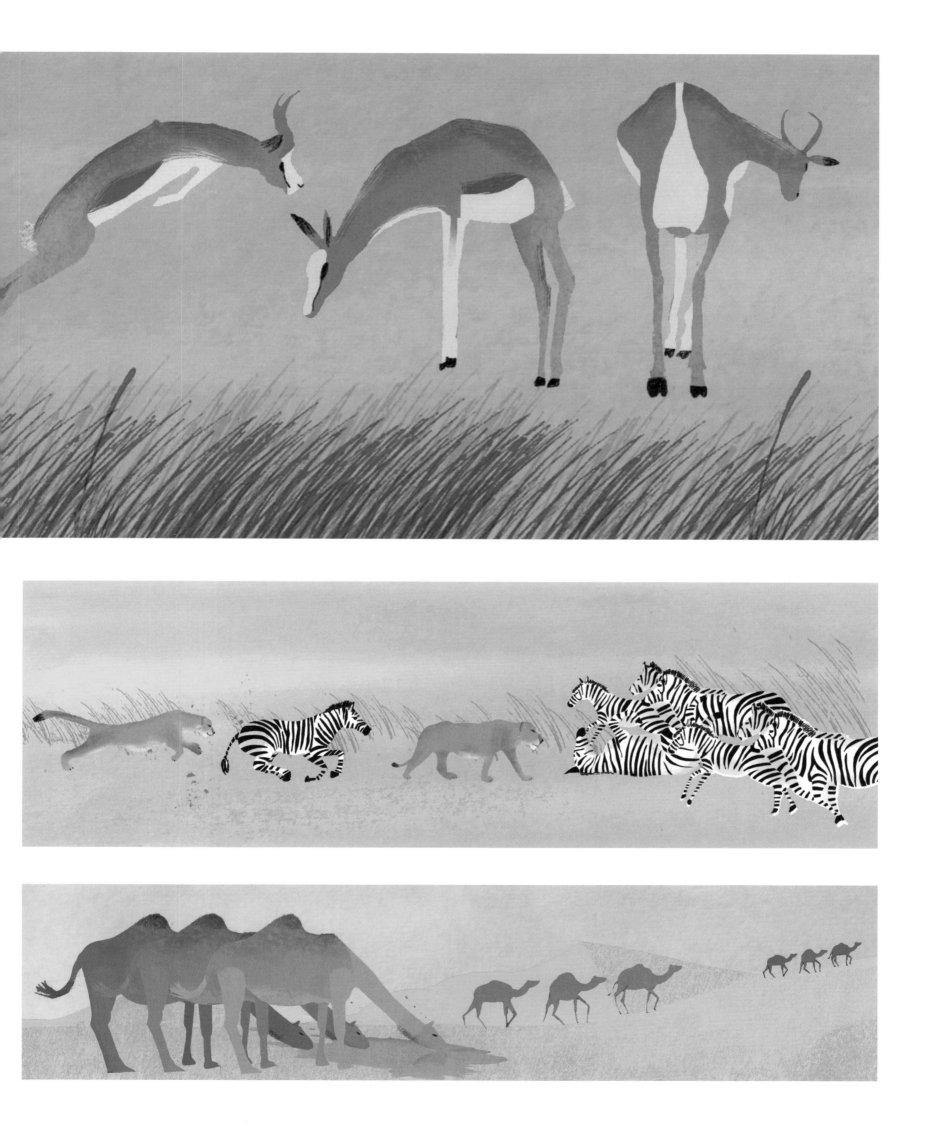

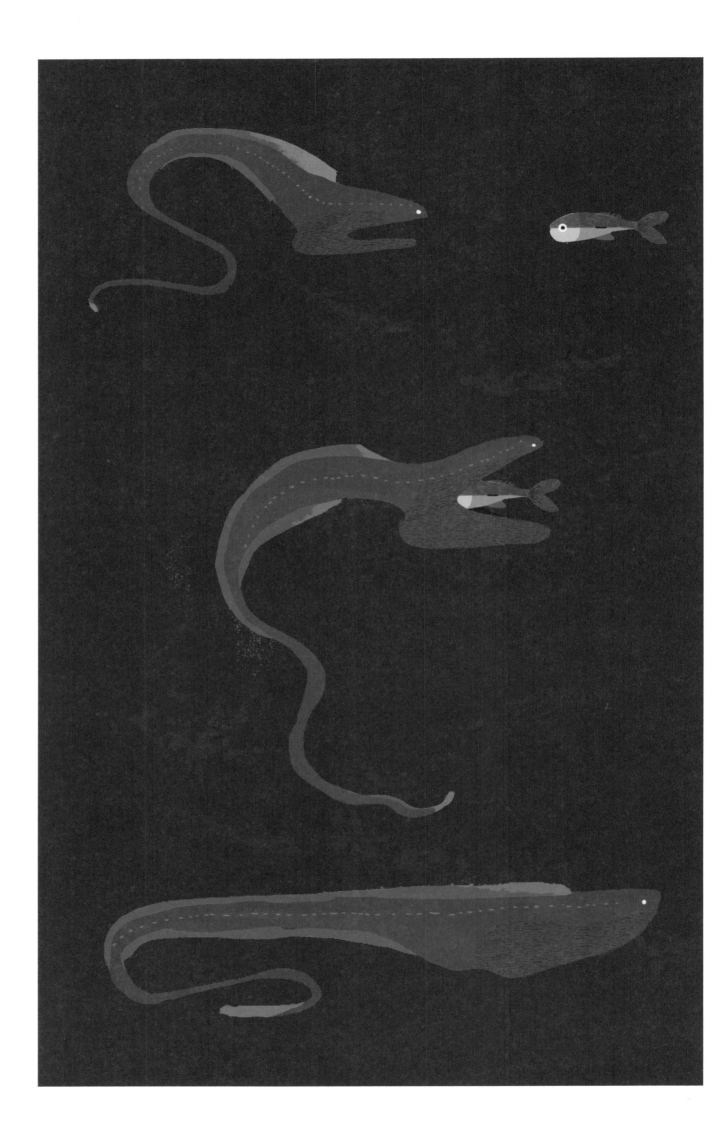

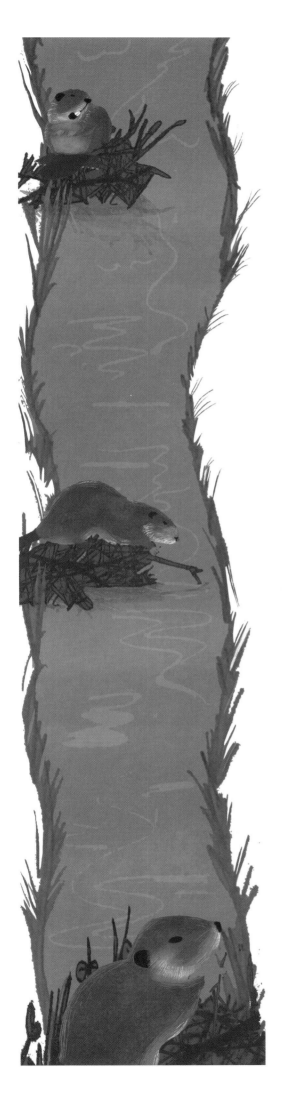

Every picture tells a story....

Two birds meet and build a nest....

In the autumn, hedgehogs find a winter home... and hibernate until the arrival of spring.

A dandelion's seeds are carried on the wind and dispersed, until eventually more dandelions grow.

Mole uses his sharp, curved claws to dig an underground home called a burrow.

A butterfly begins life as a caterpillar, becomes a chrysalis... and finally a beautiful butterfly.

Many oak trees begin to grow when a squirrel forgets where he buried his winter store of acorns.

A frog begins life as frogspawn, then becomes a tadpole and finally a frog.

A combination of sun and rain at the same time often results in a rainbow.

Oak trees grow from a tiny seed called an acorn.

A wild boar uses his long snout to forage for food.

Woodpecker pecks a hole in a tree trunk and uses his long, barbed tongue to find food.

The wild horses of the Camargue, France, change color as they grow, eventually turning white.

A ladybug begins life as an egg, which becomes a larva, then a pupa... and finally a ladybug.

A fire salamander releases poison from his pores to fend off a predator.

The seasons of the year are spring, summer, autumn, and winter.

A cuckoo lays her egg in another bird's nest.

A scout ant leaves a pheromone (scent) trail to lead his colony to food.

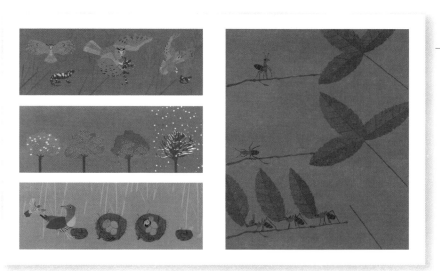

A shrew eats 80–90% of its body weight in food daily.

A caribou warns the herd of danger by releasing a scent from special glands in her ankle.

A snow leopard wraps his long tail around himself like a scarf to keep warm.

A large swarm of mosquitoes can turn the sky gray.

Musk oxen huddle together to keep warm in the snow.

An ermine's fur turns white in winter to camouflage her in the snow.

Swans meet and mate for life.

The lunar cycle is 29.53059 days. (And wolves don't really howl at a full moon.)

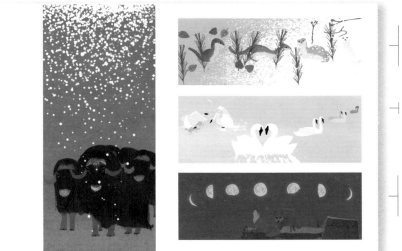

Orangutans sometimes use a palm leaf as a makeshift umbrella.

A slow loris hangs from a tree branch to eat.

A tiger's stripes mean he is well-camouflaged when hunting.

A panda spends almost all of her time eating bamboo... and sleeping.

Dung beetles push along a ball of poop before burying it.

When a king cobra is threatened, he raises his head and spreads out his hood.

A volcano smolders and smokes before lava erupts.

A peacock fans out his tail feathers to attract a peahen.

Proboscis monkeys bellyflop into the water, where their webbed feet help them to swim.

A crocodile basks unseen, before leaping up to attack its prey.

A snake regularly sheds his skin.

A baby koala senses his way from his mother's pouch onto her back.

A scorpion injects venom from his tail into his prey.

A bat uses sonar to navigate his way into a cave.

When startled, a kangaroo joey may jump headfirst into his mother's pouch.

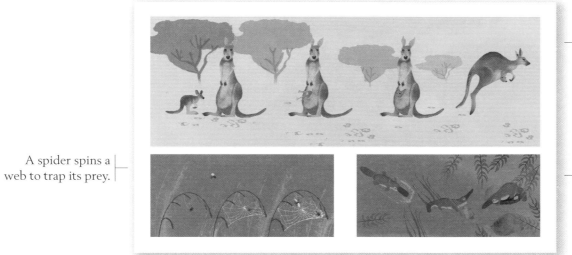

A spider spins a web to trap its prey.

The duck-billed platypus is one of only two types of mammal that lay eggs.

The anglerfish lures small fish with her luminous "lamp," then swallows them up.

Sea horses change color as they perform a courtship dance.

A turtle lays her eggs in a hole in the sand before returning to the sea.

A puffer fish inhales water and inflates to three times his normal size when under attack.

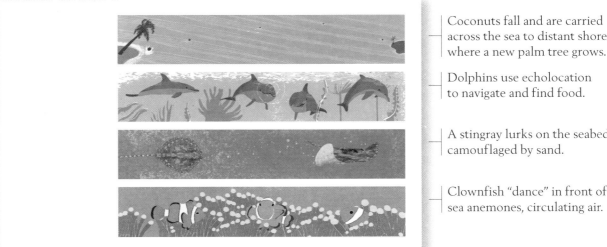

Coconuts fall and are carried across the sea to distant shores, where a new palm tree grows.

Dolphins use echolocation to navigate and find food.

A stingray lurks on the seabed, camouflaged by sand.

Clownfish "dance" in front of sea anemones, circulating air.

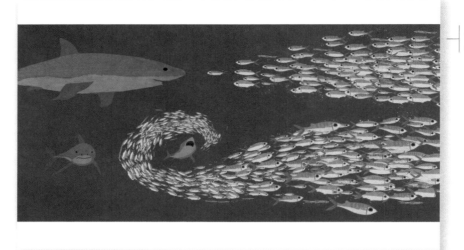

A shark scares off a shoal of small fish.

A female snow petrel flies at high speed while her mate tries to keep up.

Gentoo penguins "propose" by dropping a pebble at a female's feet.

An Antarctic shag feeds fish to her chicks.

A seal can dive up to 3,000 ft (914 m) into the ocean.

The albatross has the largest wingspan of all birds at around 11 ft (3.35 m).

Baleen whales work in pairs, blowing bubbles to alarm and catch krill.

A meerkat stands guard, watching for predators.

A giraffe uses her long neck to feed from the highest branches.

The lion lives in a pride and is the only "sociable" big cat.

A warthog has a varied grooming routine.

The ostrich is the fastest two-legged creature, reaching speeds of 43 mph (70 kph).

The cheetah is the fastest land animal, running at speeds of up to 70 mph (113 kph).

A springbok can jump up to 13 ft (4 m) in the air.

Elephants try to help an injured member of the herd back onto her feet.

Zebras band together to protect one of their wounded.

Camels can drink up to 30 gallons (135 liters) of water in 15 minutes.

The blue whale is the largest animal on Earth.

A squid squirts ink to foil an attack from a swordfish.

A crab hitches a ride through the ocean on a sea jelly.

The gulper eel has a huge mouth to gobble up his prey.

A cuttlefish changes color to match his background.

Narwhals cross tusks in a pretend sword fight.

Sea slugs display a huge array of colors and patterns.

An octopus uses a coconut shell to hide from predators.

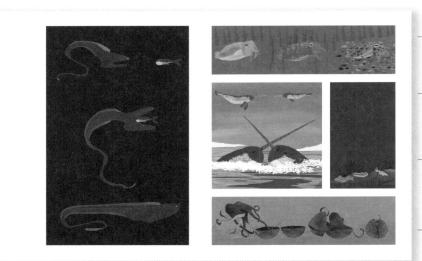

A leopard keeps his dinner safe from circling hyenas by climbing a tree.

The chameleon is a master of disguise.

A tree frog uses the sticky pads on his hands and feet to cling on.

The Venus flytrap senses a fly and…snap!

A parrot makes her home in the jungle canopy.

An armadillo has a fail-safe defense when in danger—it curls itself into a ball.

A praying mantis grabs her prey with lightning speed.

Baboons help each other with their grooming.

Llamas often spit at an unwelcomed visitor.

A tarantula shoots tiny barbs at his attacker.

Bees collect pollen from plants and flowers.

A salmon swims downriver to the sea, then returns to lay her eggs.

A moose's antlers are fully grown by September.

Bald eagles clasp talons in a cartwheel display.

A beaver builds a dam.

Seeds need sun and rain to grow into corn.

The oldest giant sequoia tree is about 3,500 years old.

A hummingbird uses her long tongue to lap nectar from flowers.

An Arctic hare's fur changes color with the seasons.

A walrus uses his tusks to break through the ice.

An Arctic fox has such good hearing that he can hear prey underneath the snow.

The polar bear's home is threatened as the ice melts.

The Aurora Borealis is a spectacular light show.

A snowy owl defends her young against predators.

Our birds' eggs hatch and the babies leave the nest....

What do *you* think that story is?